DATE DUE			

WARTHOGS

WARTHOGS

DON P. ROTHAUS

THE CHILD'S WORLD

In the lazy afternoon sunshine on the plains of Africa, tourists with binoculars and cameras marvel at the herds of animals roaming the grasslands. Lions and other predators are sometimes visible lying beneath the shade of large trees. Then, from near a patch of thorny brush, an unusual animal trots away followed closely by four of its babies. It is the wild pig of Africa, more commonly known as the warthog.

The warthog is one of the most bizarre looking animals of the African plains! It gets its name from the four wartlike bumps on its long, flat face. Scientists have suggested many explanations for these unusual bumps. Some scientists say that they provide protection for the eyes and face during pushing matches with other warthogs. Others say that they are another weapon the warthog uses, along with its long tusks, when it defends

itself against predators. Another theory is that the bumps protect the face and eyes when the animal is forced to graze for grasses underneath thorny bushes during the dry season. During these dry spells, thorns accumulate on the bumps, making them look more like pincushions than warts. Whatever the reason for the bumps, they certainly turn the warthog into an odd-looking animal!

A relative of the pig, the warthog has many other distinguishing features, including two sets of tusks. The short pair are razor sharp and covered with a hard enamel that keeps them sharp. The long pair are only tipped with enamel, so they become dull as the animal grows older.

The warthog's head is long, flat, and wide. Its body is fat and piglike, but its legs are relatively thin. When the warthog runs, its long, tufted tail sticks straight up in the air like a little flag. When the animal is threatened, its horselike mane stands on end. A full-grown adult warthog may be thirty inches tall at the shoulders and weigh between 130 and 265 pounds! It usually measures between four and five feet in length.

The warthog is found in central, eastern, and southern Africa south of the Sahara Desert. It feeds on low-growing grasses and herbs that it finds throughout the African plains and in the open woodlands. It occasionally digs up roots, potatolike tubers, and bulbs. Because the warthog has a short neck and long legs, it must drop to its knees to eat. Since it spends so much time in this position, its knees develop leathery skin pads. The usually silent warthog makes a grunting noise while it feeds.

The warthog is particularly vulnerable to predators when it is eating. The main threat comes from lions and leopards. As it feeds, the warthog's wide-set eyes keep a constant watch for danger. The warthog also has a keen sense of smell and excellent hearing. If a predator does attack, the warthog can run away at speeds up to thirty miles per hour. Sometimes, though, it turns to face its enemy. A predator faced with the sharp tusks of a charging, angry warthog is usually quick to run away! The warthog is even more dangerous when defending its young.

Adult male warthogs live by themselves during most of the year. During the mating season, they begin long courtships with their potential mates. Each male circles and guards his partner, occasionally making a loud clanking noise. If another male comes too near, the the two males fight. These fights are simple pushing matches and seldom result in severe injury. The winner continues to court the female.

Once the female accepts the male's advances, the two animals mate, and the pregnant female gives birth 170 to 175 days later. She ventures out on her own to find a suitable den for giving birth—usually an abandoned aardvark burrow or a hollow beneath some boulders. Within the protection of the den, she gives birth to

three or four pink piglets. These small babies stay huddled within the warmth and safety of the den for two to four days. The mother leaves the den to feed, returning on occasion to allow the babies to suckle. By the end of the first week, the babies begin to venture outside the den under their mother's watchful eye. Eventually, the piglets stay with the mother continuously, returning to the den only at night.

The warthog babies and their mother form a strong bond. The whole family stays together for two to four years. This family group, consisting of a male, a female, and one to three litters, is known as a *sounder.* The young male warthogs leave the group at age two and join other young males to form bachelor groups.

If a sounder is threatened by a predator, the younger warthogs scurry quickly into the protection of the den. The last adult warthog to go into the burrow, usually a large male, goes down tail first. This keeps the animal's sharp tusks towards the entrance and prevents the predator from following the family down into the den.

The African plains can be very hot and dry. This presents a difficult problem for the warthog. Unlike some mammals, the warthog has no sweat glands to cool its body. When the warthog needs to cool off, it takes long rolls in the mud. An adult warthog is usually gray or black, but when the sun bakes the mud on the warthog's body after these mud baths, the animal may look reddish or yellowish.

It is amazing how nature can produce an animal that has the unique and bizarre appearance of a warthog. Each one of its oddities has a specific use. From the tusks it uses in defense, to the facial bumps it uses for eye and face protection, to the leathery skin pads that protect its knees while it feeds close to the ground, the warthog has adapted well to its harsh environment.

INDEX

PHOTO RESEARCH
Jim Rothaus / James R. Rothaus & Associates

PHOTO EDITOR
Robert A. Honey / Seattle

PHOTO CREDITS
TOM STACK & ASSOCIATES / Joe McDonald: front cover
Norbert Wu: 2,7,8
UNICORN STOCK PHOTOS / Rod Furgason: 4,24
Leonard Lee Rue III: 11,13,28,31
Jeff Rotman: 14
TOM STACK & ASSOCIATES / John Shaw: 17
RON KIMBALL STOCK AGENCY / Rita Summers: 18,22
Joe McDonald: 21,27

Library of Congress Cataloging-in-Publication Data
Rothaus, Don
Warthogs / Don Rothaus.
p. cm.
Includes index.
ISBN 1-56766-185-8 (lib. bdg.)
1. Warthog – Juvenile literature
[1. Warthogs.] I. Title.
QL737.U58R68 1995   95-12143
599.73'4 – dc20   CIP
                                                      AC